MEAL MASTERS
YOUR SIMPLE
GUIDE
TO MODERN-DAY
MEAL
PLANNING

MEAL MASTERS
YOUR SIMPLE GUIDE TO MODERN-DAY MEAL PLANNING

DR. MONIQUE MAY

purposely created
PUBLISHING

MEAL MASTERS
Published by Purposely Created Publishing Group™
Copyright © 2020 Monique May

All rights reserved.

No part of this book may be reproduced, distributed or transmitted in any form by any means, graphic, electronic, or mechanical, including photocopy, recording, taping, or by any information storage or retrieval system, without permission in writing from the publisher, except in the case of reprints in the context of reviews, quotes, or references.

This book is not intended as a substitute for the medical advice of physicians. The reader should regularly consult a physician in matters relating to his/her health and particularly with respect to any symptoms that may require diagnosis or medical attention.

Printed in the United States of America

ISBN: 978-1-64484-162-4

Special discounts are available on bulk quantity purchases by book clubs, associations and special interest groups. For details email: sales@publishyourgift.com or call (888) 949-6228.
For information logon to: www.PublishYourGift.com

*To the absolute joy and light of my life:
the one, the only Mitchell Ellis.*

*Son, you are truly the answer to my prayer! Thank you
for teaching me that real life doesn't read the textbook!*

*To my biggest supporters, my parents,
Tedd and Hazel May, the first guinea pigs—
I mean tasters—of my food. Thank you for being both
honest and supportive at the same time!*

*In memory of my grandmother, Louise Anders,
for being the true inspiration for this undertaking.
Thank you for planting the seed which is still
growing strong!*

"It always seems impossible until it's done."

—Nelson Mandela

"If you think you can do a thing or think you can't do a thing, you're right."

—Henry Ford

TABLE OF CONTENTS

Introduction 1

CHAPTER 1:
Meal Prep Mindset 9

CHAPTER 2:
Why Eating Healthy Is Important 17

CHAPTER 3:
Why Exercise Is Important 29

CHAPTER 4:
How to Eat Right and Make Healthy
Food Choices 35

CHAPTER 5:
Meal Options: DIY, Eating Out, and Meal
Delivery Service 47

CHAPTER 6:
How to Choose the Best Meal Delivery
Service for You 55

CHAPTER 7:
Meal Prepping at Home: How to Shop for Food and Get the Most Out of Any Recipe 65

CHAPTER 8:
Demystifying the Ideal Pantry and Freezer 75

CHAPTER 9:
Choosing the Correct Appliances and Gadgets to Get the Job Done 85

CHAPTER 10:
Storage Essentials 93

CHAPTER 11:
Meal Prep and Planning Tips and Shortcuts that Save Time and Money 99

Afterword 109

About the Author 111

INTRODUCTION

I come from a long line of women who cook, and cook well, on both my mother's and father's sides of the family. Among them all, my mother, grandmothers, and aunts have fed countless family members, friends, church members, school students, and others. My earliest memory of creating food (I don't know if it quite qualified as "cooking") is as a little girl, using my Easy Bake Oven to make a little yellow cake that came with the oven. Around the age of twelve, I tried my hand at scrambled eggs and hamburgers (thankfully not in the same meal). To this day, my father jokes that that was the first time he acted as a guinea pig for my cooking and still laughs about the eggshells that were in the scrambled eggs I served him. All these years later, my mother insists that that hamburger was the best one she has ever had *in her entire life*.

Over the ensuing years as I attended college, pursued a medical degree, trained, and then began my career as a physician, I did not always have the time or desire to cook as much. I still had signature dishes for which I was known, such as my lasagna or made-from-scratch cheesecake. From time to time, I would like to pretend that I was hosting my own cooking show as I prepared meals in my tiny condo kitchen. In the many years since then, I have developed a passion for trying new recipes and creating in the kitchen. Cooking for others brings me great joy, and my contributions to work or social potluck dinners over the years have been well received, with folks usually coming back for seconds (and thirds or even fourths) and me taking home empty, nearly-clean containers. I also enjoy hosting meals at my home, and I am blessed that my parents live near my son and me, so I can cook for them often as well.

As a physician, I have always had a general idea about what foods are better for me to eat, but surprisingly, neither my medical school nor residency curricula included any significant training about specific foods and the role they play in health and disease. Over the years, I have become more purposeful in my food choices based on my own research and taste preferences. The reason I wrote this book is to hopefully educate my readers on how they, too, can make better choices when it comes to food and how they can use a variety of stress-free strategies, shortcuts, and steps to get good food in their bellies in a short amount of time. In this way, I can combine my two passions: talking about food and all things having to do with cooking and educating people about their health.

The passion to help people began early in my life. I have known since the eighth grade that I wanted to be a physician. That is when I took a science class and learned about parts of the human body: the skin, the heart, and the eye stood out the most. I was *hooked*! I knew I had to go to medical school to learn more. But even before that, I had spent so much time in and out of hospitals that they were like my second home. I was diagnosed with vocal cord polyps, which are small growths on the vocal cords. As they grew, they would make me hoarse, and more importantly, made it difficult to breathe, so they had to be removed surgically. My first surgery was when I was a year old, and from then until around age twelve, I had to have many, many operations to remove them because they kept growing back. My mother lost count after my one hundredth surgery.

Miraculously, I never had any complications, was able to stay on track with school, and graduated high school in the top five percent of my class. After college, I attended medical school, where I graduated with honors after being elected to the national honor medical society for being in the top 10 percent of my class. Upon graduation, I became the first and only physician in my family on both sides. Having chosen the specialty of family medicine, I matched to the only residency program to which I applied, located in Charlotte, North Carolina, and was named Outstanding Resident of the Year in Family Medicine during my third and final year of the program. Of course, my greatest accomplishment was having my son Mitchell in December of 2003. He was truly the best Christmas present ever!

Sadly, however, a few years before that incredibly joyful period of my life, I lost my cherished grandmother, Louise, suddenly, just a few short months after I graduated from medical school in 1996. She had just attended my medical school graduation that May and of course was proud of me. However, I could see then that her heart was getting weaker, because she could barely walk the two city blocks in Philadelphia between the locations for the graduation ceremony and reception. This was a definite decline in her condition in the four years since she had attended my graduation from college.

I will always cherish our next-to-last conversation that we had about a week and a half before she passed and just two days before she suffered a massive stroke that left her with slurred speech. I was three months into my internship and had just returned from a vacation when I called my mother to check in. Even though nothing was wrong at the time, she urged me—very strongly—to call my grandmother. After offering excuses why I could not call and saying I would call her later, I finally gave in and called her that night—and I am *so* glad I did! We had a wonderful conversation that night filled with laughter and love. I am so thankful that I took my mother's advice and called her, because the *next* time I spoke to my grandmother, she did not sound at all like herself and it was very difficult to understand her due to the slurred speech from the stroke.

The day that it happened, I was in the middle of a busy obstetrics clinic in Charlotte, North Carolina when my mother called from New York to tell me, with concern in her voice, that "Momma doesn't sound right." My grandmother was in Detroit at the time, where she was caring for her son, who himself had just had a recent stroke. Somehow, despite the severe weakness on one side of her body, she had left the hospital where she was visiting him so she could go home and drink some apple cider vinegar. Unfortunately, that was her preferred treatment for her uncontrolled blood pressure. Someone had checked her blood pressure before she left the hospital and told her it was very high. I still do not know or understand how she made it back to the house. As a physician, I of course knew that the slurred speech and weakness were signs of a stroke. When I spoke with her, my fears were confirmed and I urged her to call 911 and return to the hospital *immediately*.

A few days later, after she had been stabilized, we spoke one more final time. Her speech was permanently and severely slurred and she was now paralyzed on one side of her body. When I got the call from my mother the following week that she had passed away, barely forty-eight hours after returning home to Alabama, I just remember being in shock and disbelief. How could that have been our final conversation? I did not get to tell her good-bye. I would not get a chance to see her again. After the shock and disbelief wore off, I began to feel very angry at her. Why had she not taken better care of herself, eaten right, stopped smoking, and taken her blood pressure medicines like she should have? How could she have passed away? She was only 67 years old! I had not even had my son yet; she was supposed to be here for that! The grief was almost unbearable.

As her oldest granddaughter, I shared a special bond with my grandmother, despite my growing up in and around New York City and her living in Alabama. I just thought she was so adventurous and fun to be around. I have fond and cherished memories of visiting her as a little girl and spending time with her in the kitchen, drinking coffee with her (she would make mine with a lot of cream and sugar, just how I like it to this day), and sometimes watching her cook. In college, I would visit her during breaks. One of my favorite recipes of hers was her "sweet bread": a plain yellow cake that she would make from scratch. It was so moist and always smelled so good, and it was best served warm right out of the oven. Since I lived so far away, I would look forward to when she would send care packages with her delicious sweet bread made just for me. Over the years, I of course have let the anger go and instead focus on my memories of her laugh, her sense of style, and how loved and cherished I felt by her when I would receive one of those delicious care packages!

I believe that my grandmother's cooking is why I enjoy cooking and creating in the kitchen so much. I am so flattered when my mother tells me my cooking tastes like her mother's. By cooking and creating, I show my family and friends how much I love and care about them, and I want to help others to do the same. I am a board-certified and licensed family physician with over twenty years of clinical experience and founder of the Physician in the Kitchen. Through my meal delivery service, cookbooks, and cooking utensils, I help people in busy households enjoy healthy eating without impacting their hectic schedules. My subscribers get to FEED: Flavorful, Efficient, Economical, and Delicious meals, and they also learn how to improve their meal prep skills. They are more productive, less stressed about meal prep, and can spend more time with loved ones and friends engaging in activities that they enjoy. I know that my grandmother is looking down from Heaven, proud that her oldest granddaughter is carrying on the tradition of delivering good food.

See you in the kitchen!

Xoxo,

Dr. Monique

CHAPTER 1

MEAL PREP MINDSET

Welcome, Dear Reader! If your email inbox is anything like mine, you have received many coaching offers to help you improve your mindset in a variety of topics, whether it be about your relationship with your significant other, with money, or even with food. After all, your brain is at the top of your body for a reason: it is the control center for everything you think, do, and are, so starting with the right mindset, or frame of mind, is key to being successful in anything you do in life. So how ironic and pathetic is it that we often give little or rushed thought to what we use to fuel the wonderful work of engineering known as the human body? Sadly, some people give more thought to the type of gas that they put in their car than they do to the type of food they eat. Anything worth doing right takes planning, and eating healthily is no different.

In this hectic, nonstop time that we live in now, we are often overscheduled, overextended, overworked, underappreciated, and sleep-deprived, and the days can seem to go by in a blur (are the Christmas decorations really being put out in July now?). Because of this, being purposeful about what we eat is crucial. When we do not give thought to what, when, and how we eat, we are more likely to eat on the run, often eating something wrapped in paper or in a box or a bag, and that can sabotage whatever health goals we may have set for ourselves. Failing to meal plan leads to making less-than-ideal choices; racking up empty calories (either in what we eat or drink); eating too much fat, salt, and processed foods; and wasting food, just to name a few issues. It can also wreak havoc on our financial budgets as well.

As I used to tell my patients during my twenty years of clinical practice: we all make time for what is important. If getting your nails and hair done every week is important to you, then you will book those weekly appointments and make sure they are locked in your phone. If exercise is important to you, then you will make time (notice I did not say *find*) to do it, whether it be 5 AM or 5 PM. You may be wondering, "Dr. Monique, what is the difference between 'finding' and 'making' time to do something?" Well, say you *find* a dollar bill while walking down the street. You did not *plan* on finding that money, you just happened to look down and there it was. But if you need to get some cash from the ATM, you *make* time to go to the bank. One is by chance, the other is purposeful. Similarly, making time for what is important in your life should include making time to plan and execute your healthy meals.

Another reason that having the correct mindset when it comes to eating is important is that it sets a good example for your children. Sadly, the rates of overweight and obese children in the United States have risen to epidemic levels, and so have the health issues associated with carrying excess weight. Doctors are seeing high blood pressure, Type 2 diabetes (which we used to only see in adults), and cholesterol problems in children now. The reasons for this surge are multifactorial and beyond the scope of this book, but socioeconomics; the elimination of physical educational requirements in schools; mass marketing of foods produced with increased hormones, additives, and chemicals; and an increase in sedentary behaviors such as playing video games are all factors. Well-intentioned parents and caregivers may also use food, snacks, or beverages as comforting or soothing measures, bribes, or rewards, causing children to make that association throughout their lives. Instead of just eating when they are hungry, they are then more likely to eat when they are sad, happy, angry, or bored and fail to recognize natural cues such as satiety (in other words, to stop eating just before or when they are full).

An offshoot of mindset is mindfulness. According to Lexico.com, mindfulness is defined as the "quality or state of being conscious or aware of something." Another way to think of this is just being "present." This is especially important during mealtime. When one is multi-tasking while eating, he or she is not paying attention to what is being eaten, and that can lead to overeating. This was made crystal clear to me a few years ago with a personal experience that I had. I had purchased a candy bar and then ate it while I was driving. By the time I had driven a relatively short distance, I looked down and the candy bar was gone! I knew I had eaten it because I was holding the empty wrapper in my hand and there was no one else in the car (sadly I could not blame that one on my son), but I had no memory of eating the entire thing because I had been driving and listening to the radio at the same time. What a waste of a couple hundred calories!

Eating at the table, away from the distraction of the television or cell phones, allows one to recognize cues such as satiety (or the feeling of fullness after a meal) and decreases the risk of overindulging. It also allows for valuable family time, where parents can connect with their children and significant others can connect with each other after a long and busy day. In this day and age of instant gratification and constant overstimulation, it can be challenging to unplug and just be present in the moment with loved ones, but doing so is very important for both physical and emotional reasons.

Lastly, I can imagine what some of you may be thinking: what if I am not a planner? What if the thought of making checklists or grocery lists terrifies or intimidates me? What if I simply hate to go grocery shopping and hate to cook and would rather spend my time doing something else? While one, some, or all of those may be true, you can still be purposeful about how and what you eat in a way that fits your personal habits, time constraints, and budget. The key is just to acknowledge that it is important to make the best choices you can when it comes to fueling your body and commit to incorporating baby steps to make them happen. Another quote of mine from my days of practice is "you did not gain the weight/develop diabetes/high cholesterol/high blood pressure overnight, so you are not going to undo them overnight either." But with the right mindset and a few easy tips and tricks, anything is truly possible.

NOTES

NOTES

NOTES

CHAPTER 2

WHY EATING HEALTHY IS IMPORTANT

It is pretty much impossible in this day and age not to know or at least have heard about the benefits of a healthy diet and regular exercise (more on that in the next chapter). Both are beneficial for overall good health, good sleep, normal digestion and bowel habits, healthy immune function, and a good overall outlook on life. They can also help to prevent a lot of the health conditions that we physicians treat every day: high blood pressure, diabetes, heart disease, obesity, high cholesterol, and certain types of cancer, to name a few. Once someone is diagnosed with these conditions, the course or severity can be improved dramatically by lifestyle changes, and healthy food and exercise can decrease or eliminate the need for prescription medications. In addition, some inflammatory conditions such as arthritis can be improved by a healthy diet and regular exercise.

Like the saying goes, "garbage in, garbage out." To use the car example again, if you own a high-end luxury sports car, you would not put cheap gas in it and expect it to perform up to its fullest potential. Well, the human body works the same way. I am sure you can think of certain foods, that, when you eat them, leave you feeling sluggish, mentally hazy, bloated, and just plain blah. That is because they offer no nutritional value whatsoever and instead are filled with empty calories and harmful additives. A good rule of thumb is that you should be able to read, recognize, and pronounce the ingredients listed on the packaging in which your food is packaged. If you cannot, do yourself a favor and put it back. Not so surprisingly, one of the most beneficial aspects of fresh fruits and vegetables is that there are no labels to read.

A word about labels: in addition to the list of ingredients, a food label also has the nutritional information for each component in the food item, such as calories, carbohydrates, cholesterol, sodium, protein, and fat (including saturated and trans, which are both bad for you). The label provides you the amount of each nutrient per serving as well as how many servings there are in the package. But be careful: a serving is a defined quantity set by the manufacturer, and that may be significantly different from what you consider to be a serving size. I cannot stress enough: a serving size is *not* however much you can eat in one sitting. One noticeable exception to that rule though: if you are eating fresh fruits and vegetables prepared with no added fats, salts, or sugars, eat up. But remember: that does *not* include a salad loaded with creamy salad dressing, cheese, meats, bacon bits, and whatever other processed toppings you may want to add.

For example, if a label on a box of cereal says a serving is one *half* cup and it contains 150 calories per serving, but you eat one *whole* cup instead, you have just consumed 300 calories instead of 150 calories. The same multiplication must be done for all of the components. If the sodium per serving is listed as 40 mg and you eat two servings, then you have consumed 80 mg of sodium. These calculations are important to know if you are trying to stay within the recommended daily allowances for calories, carbohydrates, sodium, and other nutrients.

Keep in mind that the average healthy adult should eat about 2000 calories and about 1500 mg of sodium per day. Too much sodium increases blood pressure and puts a strain on the heart, increasing the risk for heart attacks. It can also increase the risk for swelling in your hands and feet. The daily recommended breakdown for each nutrient is as follows: carbohydrates 45-65 percent of total calories, protein 10-35 percent of total calories, and fat 20-35 percent of total calories. For fats, you want to choose unsaturated versus saturated or trans fats, since the latter can raise your cholesterol levels, contribute to heart disease, and increase the risk for heart attacks.

In order to determine how many grams of each you should eat each day, remember that carbs and protein each have four calories per gram and fat has nine calories per gram. So using our daily goal of 2000 calories total, that equals 225-325 grams of carbs (doing the math: 2000 x 45 percent = 900, and 2000 x 65 percent = 1300, for a range of 900-1300 calories from carbs per day. You then divide both 900 and 1300 by four to get 225 and 325, respectively, for a range of 225-325 grams of carbs per day), 50-175 grams of protein, and 45-78 grams of fat per day. (I will leave you to do the math for protein and fat if you so choose.) If you are trying to lose weight, these numbers would need to be adjusted down from a total of 1500 calories per day. Of course, those with health challenges such as high blood pressure; diabetes; heart, kidney, or liver disease; HIV; or cancer will need to work closely with their physician and dietician to reach whatever nutritional goals they have.

Not only is a healthy diet important for the reasons given above, but it is also good for your sex life as well. Did you know that eating certain foods helps to increase sexual performance for both men and women? Inflammation and oxidation are processes that are harmful to our bodies and can negatively impact one's sexual performance. Most if not all of the foods listed below help to decrease inflammation throughout the body and have antioxidant effects, which help to protect the body from harm and damage due to radiation, sunlight, smoke, and pollution and in turn can help improve one's sex life.

So what should you be putting on your grocery list to get it cooking in the bedroom? Oysters are a well-known aphrodisiac due to their zinc concentration, which your body uses to make testosterone, a hormone important in both men's and women's libido and sexual performance. But did you know that an avocado is a good source of omega 3 fatty acids, which are natural mood-boosters and can help you get ready for bedroom action? Remember, the brain is the largest sex organ, so boosting natural mood enhancers is a great way to start. Asparagus has high levels of the B vitamins B6 and folate, which can boost arousal and orgasm.

Nuts are a healthy snack option and can boost sexual performance as well. Just three to four handfuls of pistachios a day can improve erectile dysfunction (ED) significantly in about three weeks. Eating nuts can also help women who have high cholesterol levels in just three weeks. They may suffer from decreased libido, difficulty with lubrication and having orgasms, and decreased sexual satisfaction due to high cholesterol. Women may also have clitoral dysfunction from blockages of the pelvic arteries, making it difficult to achieve orgasm.

Nitric oxide (NO) is a chemical released by the body in response to sexual stimulation. NO helps men get erections when they are sexually stimulated by relaxing the muscles in the penis that allow the chambers of the penis to fill with blood. This effect was noticed when a now-famous medicine for ED was accidentally discovered. It was initially being developed as a medicine for angina, or chest pain, due to blocked heart arteries. Researchers discovered it had this interesting "side effect," so they decided to market it for erectile dysfunction instead, and the rest is pharmaceutical history.

As an important side note, men with ED should have their hearts checked by their doctors and not just chalk it up to "aging." If the arteries to their penises are clogged up, there is a good chance that the same is happening to the arteries in their hearts due to blockages. The smaller arteries in the penis may be affected first, but over time, the larger arteries in the heart may become blocked, which can lead to a heart attack or sudden cardiac death (or dying suddenly from a heart attack). These men should get either a heart tracing called an electrocardiogram (EKG); a stress test to see how well the heart handles vigorous exercise; a cardiac calcium score, which checks to see if there is calcium clogging the arteries that supply the heart; or a cardiac catheterization, in which a cardiologist injects dye into the groin to check the heart arteries for blockages, depending on their other risk factors for heart disease, such as obesity, cigarette smoking, high cholesterol, high blood pressure, diabetes, or a strong family history of heart disease.

Foods that increase NO levels include beets, garlic, dark chocolate, and leafy green vegetables like spinach, arugula, cabbage, and kale. Other nitrous oxide-boosting foods include citrus fruits such as oranges, lemons, and limes (they contain vitamin C, which enhances levels of NO), pomegranate (which has antioxidants), nuts and seeds, watermelon (which can also decrease blood pressure), and red wine.

For men who are trying to conceive, be sure to increase your intake of walnuts. They increase sperm vitality, as does eating bananas, greens, and other vegetables like asparagus, which are full of antioxidants and help to increase sperm counts. Foods high in zinc can also have a positive impact on sperm count and women's ovaries as well, which is where the female hormones estrogen and progesterone and even the male hormone testosterone are made. It is also important to avoid tobacco and excess alcohol, tight underwear, and spending time in hot tubs.

Now that you have a better idea of which foods are good for your sex life, let's plan an ideal date night dinner menu. Be sure to avoid dairy, red meat, and heavy meals; these can cause gas, bloating, and fatigue. Keep it light and healthy. For an appetizer, there are many choices, but one of my favorites is guacamole because it is made from avocadoes. Oysters are an option for some, but a word of caution for those with weakened immune systems due to cancer, diabetes, HIV, or steroids: it is best to avoid oysters in order to prevent a foodborne illness, which can cause severe vomiting and diarrhea—the ultimate date night mood killers.

Another favorite dish of mine is a watermelon, tomato, and arugula salad with fresh mint and feta cheese. I recommend multicolored grape tomatoes in general because red tomatoes have lycopene, which protects the skin against sun damage and prevents breast and prostate cancer; orange tomatoes have vitamin E, which helps improve skin conditions such as eczema and psoriasis; and yellow tomatoes have antioxidants, which help reverse skin aging. The mint freshens your breath for the win. For your entrée, have lightly grilled salmon (which is rich in omega-3 fatty acids) with a beet (which increases NO) risotto and asparagus, kale, or spinach with red wine. Finish it off with a dessert featuring dark chocolate dipped strawberries or a dark chocolate avocado mousse, and enjoy your evening!

NOTES

NOTES

NOTES

CHAPTER 3

WHY EXERCISE IS IMPORTANT

Exercise is beneficial in its own right: it is good for you and it makes you feel good (sore muscles the next day aside). There is just something about that "sweat equity" as I like to call it: working up a good sweat, burning calories, and knowing that you gave it your all can be very satisfying. The natural endorphins that your brain releases help to elevate your mood, and you feel like you have accomplished something. Of course, if you have any health challenges, you should see your personal physician before starting an exercise program if you have not been physically active. In general, try to get some form of exercise most days out of the week for at least 20-30 minutes. If you are just starting an exercise regimen, break it up into five- to ten-minute chunks at a time and increase as your stamina, strength, and confidence improve.

People often ask what is the best kind of exercise to do, and my answer is whatever kind of exercise you are most likely to do and keep at it. Change it up and try different things to keep from getting bored. Incorporate aerobic activity, such as swimming, cycling, or running, strength training, and some form of yoga or stretching for a well-balanced regimen. For example, if you get at least 30 minutes per day, five days a week of activities like fast-paced walking or leisurely bike riding, or 15 minutes per day, five days a week, of higher-intensity activities, such as running, taking a cycle class, or playing a game of soccer or basketball, you will achieve national recommendations for weekly activity targets. There is no need to join a high-priced gym; you are literally holding a whole treasure trove of options in your hand. There are plenty of smartphone apps and shows on cable and satellite TV that can take you through a complete workout in the privacy of your home.

All exercise need not take place in the gym. You can also take the stairs instead of the elevator, park farther away in the parking lot, and exercise during commercial breaks while watching TV. If you work from home like I do, try to get up and stretch or do something every hour.

If you have a treadmill, you may consider making a DIY treadmill desk that allows you to walk at a slow speed while you work. This is a good way to get in the recommended 10,000 steps a day. Be sure to exercise caution while doing so. Wear supportive shoes and replace your shoes when the tread starts to wear down, just like you do the tires on your car. This is especially important if you run or jog several times a week.

The important thing is to just get moving, be consistent, and celebrate your wins, no matter how "small." If your goal was to exercise three times a week and you actually did it, pat yourself on the back and then set a new realistic goal. If you are trying planks for the first time and can only hold it for five seconds, that is okay. Just gradually add on five seconds at a time, and before you know it, you will be holding a plank for a full minute. The human body is an amazing work of engineering, and as we know from watching elite athletes and dancers, there are almost no limits to what it can do. Again, a positive mindset plays a key role in what you can achieve.

NOTES

NOTES

NOTES

CHAPTER 4

HOW TO EAT RIGHT AND MAKE HEALTHY FOOD CHOICES

Now that we have discussed why eating healthy is important, how do we turn that knowledge into action? If you are like a lot of Americans, you may have learned a lot of unhealthy, harmful, or detrimental eating habits starting in childhood, as I mentioned earlier. If that is so, it will take a while to unlearn those behaviors and replace them with ones that are better for you. Setting small, realistic goals is very important because it allows you to recognize that change takes time, and decreases the risk for and impact of failure. Even when—not if—you have a setback, you are more likely to get back on track faster if you focus on identifying what you need to correct and keep going. Beating yourself up and feeling defeated will turn a momentary lapse into a complete backslide.

I am going to be real with you, Dear Reader, and just go on record as saying, that in my professional opinion, "diet" is a four-letter word when it is used to mean a brief change in one's eating habits to result in weight loss. Just about any fad diet will result in weight loss (no matter how crazy and nutritionally unsound it may be), but the issue of gaining the weight back once the diet is over is often compounded with even more weight gain than where the dieter started. In addition, that setback can lead to feelings of failure and depression, because one failed to live up to his or her unrealistic expectations. This can lead to an unhealthy cycle of "yoyo-ing," where one loses and gains weight repeatedly without maintaining an ideal weight for long, followed by negative thoughts and hopelessness. The key is to make small changes that you can maintain over time for long-term success.

A great example of someone making effective lifestyle changes is the patient I had who lost 150 pounds without starting a crazy diet, having surgery, or taking any pills. You read that correctly: 150 *pounds*! Guess how he did it? Basically by doing the *opposite* of everything he had done to gain the weight. He was a truck driver, and over the years, the long hours on the road, not exercising, and eating junk food from truck stops and fast food restaurants had taken their toll. He made the conscious decision (read: changed his mindset) to improve his habits. He began packing his food and keeping it in a cooler in his cab, and he would take the time at delivery stops or fueling stops to walk and do other exercise. Sure enough, the weight melted away, and he had a new lease on life. He became an active, vested participant in his health, starting with the realization that he could make a change, and his body fell in line. Similarly, the tips in this book are meant to help the reader be efficient, purposeful, economic, and intentional in her meal planning and food intake and therefore prevent any self-defeating actions and outcomes when it comes to her health.

Eating whole fruits, vegetables, and grains are ideal because you get the most vitamins, minerals, fiber, and protein from them without artificial coloring and chemicals. Also important is to "eat your colors": try to incorporate a variety of the beautiful fruits and vegetables you find in the produce aisle in the grocery store. For example, instead of white potatoes, try purple or sweet potatoes. Instead of white cauliflower, you can cook a yellow cauliflower the same way. Dark leafy greens are more nutrient-rich than lighter greens, so choose more spinach, kale, collards, and Swiss chard when shopping. If eating these vegetables gives you gas, start low and go slow. Eat small amounts and gradually increase your intake as your system becomes accustomed to them.

Processed foods are less than ideal because the beneficial parts of the food are removed and are usually replaced with salt, sugar, and other additives or preservatives, which are often harmful. For example, brown rice is better than white rice because white rice is the processed form and has much fewer nutrients than the more natural brown rice. For those who eat meat, poultry, and fish, leaner cuts of meat and poultry and wild-caught fish are preferred. Farm-raised fish may have higher levels of contaminants and disease.

If you cannot get fresh foods, choose frozen over canned foods when possible due to the higher salt content that canned goods tend to have. This is due to the preservative effects of salt, which has been known for thousands of years. Freezing is a healthier way to preserve foods. If you must you use canned goods (I use canned beans rather than dry), just be sure to rinse them off before using them, and then prepare your meal without adding extra salt because there will be some left.

So now that we know what to eat, how do we determine *how much* of it to eat? We have talked about serving size previously. Serving or portion size is an important concept in meal planning. In general, if there are no package labels on which to rely, a portion of something is about the size of a standard deck of cards or the palm of your hand. This is particularly true for foods such as carbs, meat, poultry, and fish. However, when making your plate, feel free (and I recommend) that you pile on as many vegetables as you like. In fact, at least half of your plate should be plant-based. Within each category of carbs, proteins, and fats, there are many recommendations online about how many servings of each food group to eat each day. In general, if you eat a variety of foods such as fruits and vegetables, legumes, whole grains, nuts (including nut butters such as peanut or almond), and spices, and drink beverages such as water, tea, or coffee (not juices or sodas), you should be fine. Again, for those who eat meat, poultry, or fish, choose the healthiest options you can.

A quick word about *how* you prepare your food: air-frying, baking, boiling, roasting, sautéing, steaming, stir-frying, and broiling are all preferred to deep-frying, excessive grilling, and cooking with animal fats. Believe it or not, microwaving is thought to be the healthiest way to cook because the shorter cook time lessens the chance of damaging the healthy nutrients in the food. A lot of these methods eliminate the need to use oil. However, when oil is required, olive oil is generally preferred over vegetable oil, but other oils such as flaxseed, grapeseed, and sesame oils are good as well. If you are cooking at higher temperatures, avocado oil is preferred over olive oil.

Now that you have this delicious, well-planned, and correctly portioned plate, what do you wash it down with? Water, water, and more water. Did I mention water? A lot of us may not get enough water during the day, and when we feel hungry, we don't realize our bodies actually need water, not food. We often misinterpret our thirst for hunger. News flash: by the time you feel thirsty, you are already pretty dehydrated. So the next time you feel hungry, drink eight ounces of water first, and wait 30 minutes. You may no longer feel hungry and will have saved yourself unnecessary calories. Think of it this way: each sip of water is like a side effect-free diet pill that helps you feel full sooner and helps you to eat less and lose weight as a result. How awesome is that? Take my word for it; after all, I am a doctor, right? Keep in mind that water intake comes from a variety of sources. Foods with higher water content such as watermelon (surprise!), oranges, zucchini, cantaloupe, and cucumbers help to contribute to your daily water intake as well.

Other beverages in moderation can be good for you too. Red wine has antioxidants, which, as was mentioned earlier, help reverse the harmful effects of "free radicals," which are harmful products your body makes in response to things to which it is exposed, such as foods, sunlight, and pollution. A glass of red wine a few times a week may also help protect you from having a heart attack. Coffee can actually be beneficial for you and has been shown to decrease the risk for depression and liver cancer. Tea, especially green or black tea, contains antioxidants as well. Be aware that since both coffee and tea contain caffeine, they have diuretic effects, which means they can make you urinate more often. Be sure to adjust your water intake to make up for that. Lastly, try to minimize, or better yet, eliminate, fruit juices and sodas, which are full of artificial sweeteners, sugar, and empty calories. Soda has been linked with increased cancer rates. Even juices that claim to be 100 percent fruit juice can have excess sugars and calories and not enough of the beneficial vitamins, minerals, and fiber that the whole fruits contain.

If you, like me, think water can be a bit boring at times, spruce it up with slices or chunks of fresh fruit (such as lemons, limes, oranges, pineapple, and berries), fresh herbs (like mint or basil), or cucumber slices. Or you can drink sparkling water. This is a great way to get extra fiber, antioxidants, minerals, and vitamins along with your water. You may be wondering: what about artificial sweeteners? A word of caution about artificial sweeteners: it is probably best to avoid them, but if you cannot, use them sparingly. Some of them, such as sorbitol (found in chewing gum, for example), can cause increased intestinal gas and bloating, loud stomach rumbling, and even diarrhea (or the "bubble guts," as one of my patients called it) when taken in excess. Aspartame, another popular one, should not be taken by people who have a rare condition called phenylketonuria (PKU) and those who take medicine for schizophrenia. Lastly, as of this writing, the jury is still out on whether aspartame causes cancer or seizures.

NOTES

NOTES

NOTES

CHAPTER 5

MEAL OPTIONS: DIY, EATING OUT, AND MEAL DELIVERY SERVICE

Let's face it: life comes at you fast. And sometimes, despite our best efforts, we miss the mark and cannot always cook or prep our food the way we intended. When that happens, it is okay! Take a deep breath, assess your options, and make the best choices based on what we have discussed so far. There will be times where in one week you may cook something you planned, eat at a restaurant, *and* use a meal delivery service. After all, variety is the spice of life, and when you think about it, you have to eat at least 365 meals a year (of course if you eat three meals a day that number jumps up to 1,095!), so that is *a lot* of meal planning. It is alright to outsource from time to time. When you do have to eat a meal that you did not prepare, try to choose wisely based on the recommendations previously discussed. And a cheat day every now and then is not a fatal error either.

Let us look at each option in detail and examine the pros and cons for each. When planned properly, meals that you plan and cook at home have very few downsides. Cooking at home allows you to control the salt and fat content, saves money if you shop in bulk or with coupons (more on that later), and if you live with a significant other or children, can be a fun exercise with something to do for everyone. You can have fun and experiment, try new recipes, and make them your own based on your family's taste and dietary preferences. Downsides include the time required to shop for food, and time-consuming recipes can be difficult to prepare on a busy school night. A lot of grocery and wholesale stores now offer the option of ordering online and either curbside pick-up or delivery. Almost all recipes include the time it takes to make the dish, so you can budget your time accordingly.

When it comes to eating out, the convenience of having someone else cook can be ideal. If you call in and place a take-out order in advance, it can be ready when you get there. However, that convenience can come at a cost: entrees can be loaded with fat, salt, and excess calories, even when you think you are choosing the healthy option. If you are on a financial diet as well, eating out can often work at odds to what you are trying to achieve.

But there is one surefire way to get more value for your money *and* save calories when eating out: when you order your meal, ask the server to bring a to-go box when your food is served so you can put half of your food in it *before* you even start eating. Some restaurants serve much more than dietary recommended portion sizes, and you can easily get two meals for the price of one. Removing the extra food before you start eating allows you to pay attention to satiety cues that help you stop eating sooner instead of eating until you are stuffed and *then* placing what's left in the box. When you do the latter, you are more likely to overeat. Drinking eight ounces of water before a meal also helps you eat less as well. Fortunately, there has been an increase in the number of restaurants that offer truly healthier and plant-based options with fewer hidden ingredient bombs. "Ingredient bombs" are ingredients found in foods that may be hidden or in excess of recommended daily intake (think: salt or sugar).

Lastly, the rise in meal delivery services speaks to the need for quick and easy options for dinner. There are a variety of options, including vegetarian and vegan, and come premade or give you the option of following a recipe card and cooking the meal yourself. Just like cooking from scratch, they also allow a family to bond in the kitchen and can be educational and fun for little ones as well. The downsides include the costs, with some subscribers stopping after just a few weeks. The other negative is the effect on the environment with the excess packaging that each order generates. Some have too many steps to be completed in a short amount of time. Finally, some plans only offer options that feed two or four people, which is not ideal for singles, and some of the ingredients may arrive in less-than-ideal shape or freshness.

To summarize: it is okay to use a variety of methods to feed your family. You just need to stay mindful of what you are trying to achieve, whether it be healthier eating, saving time, sticking to a budget, trying new foods and expanding your palate, or all of the above. For the most part, meals that you prepare at home would be the ideal, but if you have to supplement with help from a meal delivery service or a restaurant, that should be the exception and not the norm. Set a goal for the week and reward yourself for each week that you stayed true to your plan. A small token like a healthy snack in the form of a piece of fruit or something new from the produce aisle or a massage (my favorite!) every now and then can be the best reward!

NOTES

NOTES

NOTES

CHAPTER 6

HOW TO CHOOSE THE BEST MEAL DELIVERY SERVICE FOR YOU

As the Physician in the Kitchen™, I am here to help you navigate the various options available for home meal delivery plans. It is so easy, convenient, and commonplace now to order anything and have it delivered, so why not order your food this way as well? There are so many meal plan options on the market that it may be a bit overwhelming when you do decide to use one. I think the best way to approach this is to examine the reason *why* you are using a meal plan service. If it is to save time, choose one that either delivers pre-made meals that you just heat and eat, or if you have to prepare the meal, be sure it has a minimal number of steps and a small number of ingredients with clear directions on the recipe card telling you how long it will take to prepare it. You also want one that does not require a lot of cookware or dishes that will need to be washed afterwards. If it is to try a different type of diet, such as vegan or vegetarian, then choose one that offers the options you want.

If you want to save money, you will need to calculate the cost per person per meal and compare that to what you would spend if you had to shop for the ingredients yourself. If it works out that you are spending more on the meal service, you may need to rethink things. Speaking of cost, there is a wide range of price plans out there, so you need to choose one that fits in your budget and works for you. If you find that you are not using all of the food and it ends up going to waste, that means that you need to choose a smaller plan or decrease the frequency of delivery. Look for coupons and referral bonuses as well. Some plans give you money off for each person you refer to them. If you are single, it may be cost-effective if you order for two and get twice as much food (leftovers can be used for lunch). The downside is that you may get tired of eating the same things several times in a week.

Equally important is choosing meal plans that align with your health concerns and goals. If you are diabetic or have high cholesterol or hypertension, you want to choose options that are low in sugar, trans fats, and salt. Explore to see if there are low-carb, high-fiber, and low glycemic-index options. Be mindful that there can be hidden "ingredient bombs" in the sauces or seasonings as well, so read the dietary information for everything. For example, if you start noticing excessive swelling in your hands and feet after eating a meal, the sodium or salt content may be higher than advertised.

Some home meal delivery plans provide the ingredients for you to assemble and cook yourself, and others deliver a ready-made meal that just requires heating in a microwave or toaster oven. The former option is great for those who want to improve their cooking skills. The latter option is ideal for those who are really short on time or have no desire to cook at all and just want to get something delicious on the table as soon as possible. If you are using the ones that you prepare yourself, they do require that you have some basic staples in your pantry or fridge, such as olive oil or butter. You will also need to have certain utensils and cookware. Of course, that means dishes and pots to clean afterwards, while the ready-made option does not require you to dirty any dishes; just heat and eat.

Lastly, if you live in a larger metropolitan area, there may be locally owned and operated home meal delivery companies you may choose to support instead. Each may have something unique to offer, so do a little research to see what is out there. You might be surprised to find out just how many are near your geographical area. When you are comparing plans, you want to know the degree of variety and options amongst the available meal plans. When you find one you like, determine how much variety it offers, how often new meals are offered, and if they offer vegetarian or vegan options.

By now, you are now an expert on how to read a food label. Do the meals have nutritional labels that inform you about the serving sizes and calorie, fat, and sodium counts of the meals? In addition, there are many other factors to consider. How much does it cost per meal? Are there discounts for ordering in bulk or several meals at a time? Can you order a la carte, or do the meals come as a package deal? Do they offer breakfast, lunch, dinner, or all of the above? Can they tailor the meals to fit your specific nutrition plan? How often do you plan to use them and how many meals per week do they offer? Do they offer dessert options?

Check to see if they offer delivery, and if so, is there a fee or purchase minimum? If you have to pick up the food yourself, how far do you have to travel? When you factor in time and gas to get there and back, there may not be any real savings compared to something delivered to you. Is the website easy to use? How customer-service-oriented are they? Are they environmentally conscious and do they use recyclable or biodegradable packaging?

Despite all of the convenience that home meal delivery services offer, there are valid concerns about the effect that the packaging for each delivery has on the environment. While we are striving to lead healthier lives, we must also be mindful of the effect our actions have on the environment. For example, each ingredient may be individually wrapped in plastic that is not recyclable. Depending on the frequency of deliveries, this can add up very quickly. Choose companies that use more eco-friendly containers, such as cardboard and paper packaging. Be sure to recycle the ice packs, and check to see if the company offers any incentives to return them.

For those with health or medical concerns, using a meal delivery service featuring meals prepared by a physician is ideal. How wonderful would it be to order affordable, healthy, doctor-recommended meals made with local and sustainable ingredients delivered to your home in environmentally friendly packaging from a menu with variety and delicious offerings? The added convenience of just heating it up and not having to dirty extra pots and dishes is a perfect time-saving feature.

With my Charlotte-based meal delivery service, I address these concerns and provide my subscribers with well-prepared meals that take into account the health-promoting benefits of vegetables, fruits, legumes, spices, and plant-based options such as tofu and offer healthy meat, poultry, and fish options as well. Depending on your health goals and dietary preferences, a meal delivery plan prepared by a physician with expertise in healthy meal planning is a great alternative and will complement and fit in quite well with your overall plan for purposeful meal planning. Whether you choose to go with a local or national meal delivery service, make sure that it makes sense for you and what you are trying to accomplish, whether it be timewise, dietarily, or financially.

NOTES

NOTES

NOTES

CHAPTER 7

MEAL PREPPING AT HOME: HOW TO SHOP FOR FOOD AND GET THE MOST OUT OF ANY RECIPE

By now, you know why eating healthy is important and what options are available to you. Being the adventurous goal-setter that you are, you have decided you want to turn over a new leaf and give this cooking thing a try. I mean, how hard could it possibly be, right? You may want to plan and prepare a meal all by yourself, but you do not know where to start. Just like anything else, planning is key. Start with a grocery list, and be sure to stick to it. Do not go shopping when you are hungry, because you are more likely to pick up items that are not good for you and spend more money than you intended.

Have you ever noticed that staples like dairy and frozen foods are all the way in the back corner of the store and "impulse items" such as sodas, chips, and candy are up front at the register? That design is deliberate—so that you have to walk through almost the entire store to get some of the basic items you need. That increases the likelihood that you will pick up less-than-ideal options. I suggest you start shopping in the produce aisle, which is usually on the right side of the store as you enter. The worst that can happen there is that you pick up an extra piece of fruit or a new vegetable that you haven't tried yet. Either way, it's a good thing! I actually enjoy smelling and squeezing the produce myself to get the best one for whatever exciting recipe I am going to try next. Finding surprise sales on items I was going to buy always make me feel like I'm winning as well.

Just like so many things in modern life, there are so many options on where to shop. Yes, there is the traditional grocery store, but there are also farmer's markets, wholesale clubs, and online services. Farmer's markets are a wonderful way to get seasonal produce and other locally produced items, often at a better price than grocery stores. You are helping to support your local community as well and may find new and interesting things to try. The items are likely to be fresher, since they traveled a shorter distance and may actually taste better than what you can buy in a grocery store. There may be more organic options offered as well. In addition, there can be health benefits to eating local foods. For example, locally produced honey can be purchased at farmer's markets and can be a natural, medication-free way to treat seasonal allergies. By ingesting local pollen, you may experience fewer allergy symptoms over time since you become more immune to it.

Wholesale clubs and online services offer you the convenience of shopping in bulk, which is usually cheaper per unit (for example pound, serving, or container) than if you bought it at the grocery store. You can also opt to have items delivered to your door, saving you precious time. You have to determine if the membership fee that the wholesale clubs charge is worth it in the long run. If you have a large family or like to cook in bulk and then freeze it, this is likely the most economical option for you. Keep in mind that your local grocery store may offer sales on bulk items, and when you factor in coupons, the savings may be greater than at a wholesale club.

Depending on what you are shopping for, you may need to be strategic on when you go shopping. For example, if you are planning a meal with seafood, you want to be sure to buy it no more than two days before you plan to use it, or you will need to freeze it immediately. Check with the store to see when their seafood is delivered so you know you are getting it fresh. Try to get it as close to the time it was delivered if possible. As for produce, depending on when the store gets its deliveries, it may be better to shop mid- to late-week for your fruits and vegetables. Be sure to check to see what items have been marked down, such as ripe bananas or mushrooms, which may be a day or two past their prime but can still be used in a recipe.

Having a food budget and sticking to it when you are shopping are crucial steps to reaching your financial and dietary goals. Checking newspaper coupons and apps that contain coupons on items you use can save you significant money at the register. Be sure to sign up for digital coupons and loyalty cards as well. This is where buying in bulk (more on this later) really adds up. But again, choose wisely: just because you can buy ten pounds of peanut butter doesn't mean you should. Only buy the items that you and your family need and that help you stay on your financial and dietary goals.

Planning a weekly menu is great because it is like a GPS: it helps you know where you are going and how to get there. If you are trying new recipes, you can plan for the week and shop accordingly, or you can "shop" your pantry and freezer and make a menu based on what you already have. Either way, there is no need to recreate the wheel if you are not that creative or adventurous or are just are pressed for time. There are countless apps, cookbooks, recipes, and blogs to help you out. Just pick something based on what you like and go from there. Do not over think it.

Once you have decided what to cook and you have all of the ingredients, be sure to assemble all the ingredients before you start. Dice, chop, sift, measure, and whatever else the recipe calls for before you begin to cook, because once you do, things tend to move quickly, and you do not want to be left scrambling for an ingredient at a crucial moment. A perfect example of this is stir frying. Stir fry is fairly simple to do, but once you start adding ingredients, it cooks quickly (making it ideal for a busy weeknight, by the way), so you want to have everything ready to go. Similarly, when making a cake, you need to have all of the ingredients measured and ready to go.

Finally, feel free to tweak any recipe for what you like or whatever food allergies you may have. For example, if a recipe calls for parsley but you (like me) are a cilantro fiend, go for it! Make it your own! If a recipe calls for two cloves of garlic but you absolutely adore the taste of fresh garlic, add it. A lot of cuisines, such as Italian, Indian, or Asian dishes, derive much of their flavor from garlic, so if you want to recreate that restaurant taste, don't be shy. If a recipe calls for one teaspoon of vanilla but you are like my mother, who believes there is no such thing as too much vanilla, have at it.

One caveat: there *can* be too much of a good thing, so I suggest you add in small increments so as not to overshoot the desired effect. For example, my father loves the taste of nutmeg, which adds a delicious layer to candied yams or my famous sweet potato pies. Too much, however, can cause an unpleasant spicy effect. A few years ago, he kept asking me to add more nutmeg. One time, I added too much. It was so "nutmeg-y" that the pie was almost inedible, in my opinion. I think he agreed. Instead of the usual two to three days it would normally take him to eat one of my pies, that one lasted over a week. Apparently, even he had reached his limit.

NOTES

NOTES

NOTES

CHAPTER 8

DEMYSTIFYING THE IDEAL PANTRY AND FREEZER

I admit: my favorite room in my house is my kitchen (shocker, right?), followed closely by the pantry. I prefer a large pantry with plenty of shelving and good lighting, but in all honesty, size does not matter. As long it is dry, cool, and well ventilated, that is what counts. Your pantry is meant to store food that has a longer shelf life and should make your meal planning and prepping easy and efficient. Based on what type of food you eat, your pantry should be filled with food items that help you achieve your dietary goals. Likewise, the freezer is for perishables that you plan to use later as well as leftovers from batch cooking you may do on the weekends.

So what do I recommend you have in your pantry? Let's start with beans, because they are economical, last a good while, are very easy to build a meal around, and are super nutritious! Everyone, and I do mean everyone, should have beans in their pantry. I prefer canned, but dry beans are actually cheaper per serving. They just usually require soaking. I, however, prefer to just open a can and (rinse and) go. Beans, part of the legume family, are rich in fiber, folate, protein, antioxidants, and minerals. They help you feel fuller and thereby help to curb appetite, which in turn leads to weight loss. They are ideal with rice and in chili, soups, stews, and black bean burgers. They can be turned into delicious dips as well. Even the potential downside of increased gas can be decreased by soaking dry beans and introducing them slowly into your diet or adding a little ground ginger to them as they cook (my mother swears by this).

Dry staples include pasta, rice, quinoa (which can be served at breakfast or dinner) and other grains, lentils, cereal, snack or protein bars, granola, flour, nuts, flour, and sugar, just to name a few. Gluten-free flours include almond and chickpea flours, and there are many others on the market as well. Instead of white sugar, you can use maple syrup or coconut sugar for healthier options. Canned goods include tomatoes (whole, peeled, diced, paste), low-sodium broths or stocks, and nut butters. I also keep bottled water and soy milk in my pantry, as well as fresh fruits and veggies that do not require refrigeration, such as apples, onions, potatoes, and garlic. Here's a tip: pay attention to what area of the produce aisle in which you found your fruit or vegetable. If it was not refrigerated in the store, then do not refrigerate it once you get it home. I have made this costly mistake with fresh basil (which is sold in the same unrefrigerated area as tomatoes and garlic in most stores) by putting it in the refrigerator at home, causing it to turn brown prematurely. Spices are a must in any kitchen, but you don't want them sitting so long that they lose their freshness.

For a busy household with children, I suggest keeping an area for "lunchbox goodies." These are healthy snacks that even little ones can help meal prep for the week and pack in their lunch box each day. They should be stored on the lower shelves so they are easy for little ones to reach. Examples include rice cakes, dried fruits, fruit roll-ups, veggie chips, air-popped chips, and fruit cups (with water, not sugary syrup). Be mindful of how they are prepared, because some may have salt or sugar additives. This helps to teach your children the importance of proper portion size, planning what he or she is going to eat, and gives them responsibility of helping to pack their lunch. They can also help label shelves or containers that organize the pantry, so that when you bring home groceries, they know exactly where they belong, thus freeing you up to do other things.

Think of your pantry as a "mini grocery store." I really enjoy trying new recipes, and what makes it even more fun for me is going to my pantry and pulling ingredients off the shelf as if I were grocery shopping. But do not feel like you have to stock your pantry overnight. As you get a feel for what your household needs, you will stock it appropriately and figure out the best places to get them. For example, if you use a lot of canned beans and tomatoes like I do, you may want to buy those in bulk from a wholesale club to save money. As you stock your pantry, be sure to set it up like a mini grocery store, grouping foods together by categories that make sense and make it easy for you to find what you need to be a meal prep rock star!

As for the freezer, it should be stocked with a variety of vegetables that can be quickly defrosted and tossed in a recipe on a busy night. Spinach, broccoli, greens, peas, and corn are my favorites. Fruits such as berries (raspberries, blueberries, and strawberries), peaches, and mangoes are excellent sources of vitamins, antioxidants, and fiber. Having some on hand year-round makes it easy to use in smoothies or in desserts. Just be sure they are not packed in sugar or syrup. Be sure to label and date your foods with stickers or permanent ink. Investing in a vacuum sealer is worth it because removing air before freezing reduces freezer burn and makes foods last longer.

If you enjoy cooking with fresh herbs but hate to waste any unused portions, I have good news for you! Fresh herbs can be frozen as well. Oregano, mint, basil, parsley, and chives are some herbs that can be frozen. Make sure they are clean and dry first, chop them as large or small as you like, and then freeze them in water or olive oil using ice cube trays. Measure out a teaspoon or tablespoon of herb before adding it to the tray so you know how much you have; this will come in handy when using them in recipes. Once frozen, remove them from the trays so they don't get freezer burn and store them in a freezer bag that you have labeled and dated. When you are ready to use them, just add them to whatever dish you are preparing; they will defrost *and* flavor your food at the same time. How cool is that?

Storing your proteins is easy as well. If you buy meat, poultry, or fish in bulk, be sure to break up the package when you get home. Separate them into smaller portions that reflect how much you tend to cook at one time. For example, break a three-pound ground beef log into three one-pound bags for quick use. Don't forget to date and label each one with permanent ink. Same goes for leftovers or cooking in bulk. Casseroles, pasta dishes, meatballs, chili, boiled eggs, soups and stews are just some of the cook-ahead foods that can be frozen and eaten later. Most foods are suggested to be frozen no more than three to four months, so I suggest checking your freezer every few weeks so you keep items in rotation to be eaten before freezer burn sets in, which can sometimes happen despite vacuum sealing.

A word about labeling: if you are using freezer bags, you can write directly on them, preferably before you put your food in them. When using containers, you can certainly get fancy labels, but plain old masking tape works just as well. Just tear off a piece and label using permanent ink and place on your container. Remember to peel it off before microwaving to prevent stickiness when you peel off the label.

NOTES

NOTES

NOTES

CHAPTER 9

CHOOSING THE CORRECT APPLIANCES AND GADGETS TO GET THE JOB DONE

In all honestly, this was probably the hardest chapter for me to write, because as the self-proclaimed kitchen gadget junkie, it was hard for me not to list every gadget in my kitchen. In my livestream videos, I usually use one of my gadgets and feature it as a "celebrity guest." For those who have seen my live feeds, thanks for watching! For those who haven't, you can watch them on YouTube. I truly love and use all of my kitchen gadgets. But I do not want to overwhelm you to the point where your eyes roll back in your head and you scream, "Enough lady! I get it; you love kitchen gadgets!" So to keep it simple, I will focus on the five that I discussed in a recent livestream, as well as a few other essentials. Having the right tool for the job is important, and these appliances and gadgets help to save time and decrease or eliminate food wasting as well.

I think that there is something very satisfying in making something yourself versus buying it in the store, plus you can control the ingredients. A food processor is key if you like to make things like pesto, pie crusts, salsa, hummus, or riced cauliflower. Be sure to get one with a smaller prep bowl so you do not have to use the larger bowl when making a smaller amount. The blades are very sharp, so exercise caution when handling them. If you do not have a food processor, a blender can work in a pinch.

Slow cookers (or crock pots) are good for making stews, one-pot meals, grits, baked beams, and ribs, just to name a few dishes. The beauty of them is that you can set it to cook in the morning, and when you get home, dinner is ready. Digital models can be programmed to stir the food for you as well. A multi-pot can be used as a slow cooker, pressure cooker, rice cooker, and yogurt maker, and can serve many other functions. They are also programmable and make cooking different types of foods very easy. The pressure cooker option can be used to break down tough cuts of meat in a short amount of time and can also be used to cook beans, vegetables, seafood, and grains.

A toaster oven is a great addition to any kitchen because it can perform many of the duties of a regular oven without warming up the whole kitchen, since it is smaller and takes less time to warm up. This is crucial during hot summer months. It can be used to warm up leftovers, such as pizza, making the crust firm instead of soggy when it's warmed in the microwave. It can be used to keep foods warm as well and makes grilled cheese sandwiches in a snap. Speaking of ovens: I recommend getting an oven thermometer that checks the actual temperature inside of your oven. True story: my oven control panel would show that it was 350 degrees Fahrenheit after just a few minutes of warming, yet my cakes would not be done after the correct baking time. It was only after ruining a few cakes that I checked the actual oven temperature with a thermometer and realized that it took much longer for my oven to actually reach 350 degrees, so I was able to adjust for that time and now my cakes come out just fine.

An air fryer is a nifty appliance that allows you to cook with little to no oil. You can make homemade

French fries, fried chicken, and fish in the basket. These are just a few things you can cook in a short amount of time. It can also be used to reheat and crisp food. If there is a dehydrator option, you can use it to make your own dried fruits, croutons, or sundried tomatoes. I use mine to make dried apple rings that I toss in a mixture of cinnamon, ginger, and light brown sugar. Delicious!

A few honorable mentions include a stand mixer, which allows you to add ingredients quickly instead of having to stop or use one hand to add them if using a hand mixer; this is crucial when making a cake. A blender is good for making healthy smoothies for breakfast or pureeing silken tofu to add to a recipe. To help produce and other foods last longer, sealing them in plastic bags with a vacuum sealer keeps them from going bad too soon. You can then freeze them and use them in your recipes as needed. For easier chopping and dicing, a good set of knives is imperative, and a mandoline slicer helps you make homemade potato chips or perfectly sliced onions, tomatoes, and other veggies. Be sure to always use the hand guard that comes with it to hold the food in place as you slice, and more importantly, to prevent serious injury to your fingers.

NOTES

NOTES

NOTES

CHAPTER 10

STORAGE ESSENTIALS

Now that you have bought, prepared, and cooked all of this delicious food how are you going to store it? You certainly do not want all of your hard work to go to waste. There are a myriad of available options. When choosing one (or several), ask yourself if it will be used in your home or a lunch box, if it is environmentally friendly, how durable it is, if it is prone to staining and odors, and of course, how much it will cost. You probably never thought you would hear a doctor say this, but air equals death, specifically when it comes to food preservation. For some foods, it is easy to see the effects of air exposure fairly quickly, such as when an avocado or an apple turns brown after you cut it. Whatever options you choose, you want to be sure they do a good job at keeping air out.

My favorite storage containers are the plastic or tempered glass containers with locking tops. They are sturdy, do not break when they are dropped (or so I have heard), and do not stain permanently when foods with turmeric or pasta sauce are stored in them. They also do not retain odors, are dishwasher compatible, are stackable and therefore space saving, and are not expensive. The locking tops do a good job of keeping air out of refrigerated foods. Because they come in rectangular, square, and round shapes, small children will enjoy using them to learn their shapes as they stack and put them away.

Other temporary food storage options include aluminum foil, plastic wrap, and wax paper. Be sure to recycle when you can. These options can also be used when freezing foods to help layer, separate, and label them. Sandwich and snack bags can also be used by children to prepare lunch snacks for the week, such as grapes and graham crackers. Mason jars are an option that can be used to make layered foods such as salads or yogurt and fruit parfaits.

Do not forget to vacuum seal items when you can, which allows for longer storage in your freezer. Casseroles and other things with low fluid content are ideal for vacuum sealing. If you invest in a vacuum sealer, you will see a pretty quick return on your investment in the savings you get from not having food go to waste anymore. Some vacuum sealers also have the option for vacuum sealing jars if you like to do your own canning.

NOTES

NOTES

NOTES

CHAPTER 11

MEAL PREP AND PLANNING TIPS AND SHORTCUTS THAT SAVE TIME AND MONEY

We have covered a lot of information thus far, and now you may be wondering how you put it all together. The good news is that there are no wrong answers. First and foremost, start with a clean slate. By that I mean a clean kitchen: dirty dishes and clutter add unnecessary stress and invite a negative element that you do not need. Plus, you may not be able to find the dishes or gadgets you need when you need them. You don't want to start off feeling frazzled or defeated before you have even had a chance to begin. Try a few of the different options I have discussed and figure out what works for you. Add, tweak, and delete as necessary. Make it your own!

As I have stated before, be intentional. Make time for your meal prepping. Pick a day of the week that works for your schedule. For example, Sunday works best for me. I choose the recipes I want to make for the week and then prepare at least three to four days' worth. If you work weekends, then choose your "weekend" to knock it out. Involve family members and make it fun for the kiddos. A glass of wine and some relaxing music add nice touches. If you are like me, you could watch a cooking show and pretend you are a contestant trying to make a meal from the items in the mystery box or critique what they are doing from the comfort of your own no-pressure kitchen.

Like much in life, simplicity is best. Keep it simple. If you have picky eaters in your home, do not spring too many new things on them at once. Try recipes that feature what they like and go from there. That being said, you certainly can find creative ways to incorporate vegetables in a dish so that they will not even notice. For example, I will often add spinach to my spaghetti sauce when I make lasagna or ziti. My son happens to like spinach, but he does not even know it is hidden in there. Same for smoothies: I will toss a handful of spinach in a blueberry smoothie to increase the fiber and nutrient content without affecting the taste. Be careful with other fruit smoothies though: spinach can turn strawberry smoothies brown, which some may find unappealing.

Next, know and grow your palate. If your favorite vegetable is broccoli, try making it different ways so that you can expand your repertoire. Also, try to buy one new fruit or vegetable each week and just taste it. If you can find a user-friendly recipe, feel free to make something with it. Start with something in the same family as something you know and love. Sticking with the broccoli example, start by trying cauliflower, since it is similar in shape and appearance. You will never know how something tastes unless you try it. I have a rule in my house that my son has to at least taste something new that I have made. In doing so, he has come to love spinach quiche, omelets, and sweet potato pie, just to name a few dishes.

Remember, in order to realize the savings you can get from buying in bulk, you want to store the food properly once you get home. Divide the larger portions into whatever size you need for your family at a time and freeze the rest (have that vacuum sealer handy). One- or two-pot dishes such as casseroles, soups, chili, and pasta dishes are all great options to cook once and eat from two to four times. Take it one step further and repurpose leftovers. Thanksgiving is not the only time this is applicable. For example, if you have leftover rice, add some chopped bell pepper, mushrooms, and broccoli and make a quick stir fry, season with garlic and ginger, and boom! No need to go to your local Chinese restaurant: you have saved money and avoided the excess sodium you would likely get from takeout.

The idea of DIY does not apply to just takeout. Whether it be riced cauliflower in a food processor or dried apple chips or rings in your oven, air fryer, or dehydrator, it is often much more economical than buying them from the store. If you do not have the tools to do that or have no desire to do so, then buying items like that in bulk would be more cost effective. But remember: making it yourself allows you to control or eliminate undesirable additives and calories. If you do purchase them instead, you just have to be sure to read the nutritional information on the package as we have discussed before in order to make an informed decision.

Cooking in batches also allows you to make several individual servings of breakfast the night before and then just warm them up in the morning as needed. Use a cupcake tin to make breakfast cups with whatever ingredients you want (mini-quiches with eggs, turkey sausage, cheese, and spinach is one possibility). Breakfast burritos with beans and scrambled eggs or tofu are a wonderful high-protein option that should stave off hunger for hours. This prevents unnecessary snacking, which in turn leads to weight gain.

Mason jars are another option that can be used to store individual servings of meals, such as salad or yogurt parfait with granola. For the salad option, just pour salad dressing on it when you are ready to eat it to keep it from getting soggy. To keep expensive produce from going bad, wash fruits and veggies as soon as you get home and place them in the fridge where they will be seen easily. For example, I have my son wash the grapes that he will be taking as a snack and divide them into five snack-sized slider storage bags for each day of the week.

Lastly, make it fun! Often people dread meal prep because they do not find it fun or enjoyable. While this is something I cannot relate to personally (what is not to like with all of the gadgets and tools in the kitchen?), I do hope the suggestions in this book are helpful. For example, have different themes based on the day of the week, such as Meatless Monday, Taco Tuesday, and Wok Wednesday. Include your kids in the meal planning, and even get them little chef's hats, jackets, and aprons. Address them as "Chef" in the kitchen. In addition to having fun and creating precious memories, you just may spark their interest in a future career as a chef.

Bottom line: know thyself. If you are new to meal prepping and the kitchen in general, take small steps and incorporate one or two ideas from this book, and then just build from there. Don't try to overhaul your whole approach, kitchen, or pantry in one weekend. It is a journey, but with a good road map and a reliable vehicle, it can be a smooth and fun ride. I truly hope this book helps you on your path!

NOTES

NOTES

NOTES

AFTERWORD

Thank you to my all of my friends over the years who have eaten and enjoyed my food and encouraged me to sell it to the masses. You are the inspiration for this book and business endeavor, and I cannot thank you enough for the laughter, support, love, and trust in me!

ABOUT THE AUTHOR

Dr. Monique May, also known as the Physician in the Kitchen, is a board-certified licensed family physician with over twenty years of clinical experience. She graduated from the University of North Carolina at Chapel Hill with a degree in psychology, obtained her medical degree with honors from Temple University School of Medicine, and completed her internship and residency in family medicine at Carolinas Medical Center (now Atrium) in Charlotte, North Carolina, where she was named Resident of the Year. Most recently, she completed a master of healthcare administration at the George Washington University School of Public Health.

In 2019, Dr. May's commitment to her community was recognized with a Physician of the Year award. Dr. May enjoys cooking, experimenting in the kitchen, traveling, exercising, reading, watching sports, and spending time with her son Mitchell. She lives in the Charlotte, North Carolina, area.

Learn more at DrMoniqueMay.com

CREATING DISTINCTIVE BOOKS WITH INTENTIONAL RESULTS

We're a collaborative group of creative masterminds with a mission to produce high-quality books to position you for monumental success in the marketplace.

Our professional team of writers, editors, designers, and marketing strategists work closely together to ensure that every detail of your book is a clear representation of the message in your writing.

Want to know more?
Write to us at info@publishyourgift.com
or call (888) 949-6228

Discover great books, exclusive offers, and more at
www.PublishYourGift.com

Connect with us on social media

@publishyourgift

www.ingramcontent.com/pod-product-compliance
Lightning Source LLC
Chambersburg PA
CBHW070954080526
44587CB00015B/2299